I
REMEMBER

I REMEMBER

Cowboy Rhyme

Copyright November 2003
All Rights Reserved

Published November 2003

Painted Word Studios Publishing

Painted Word Studios Publishing
P.O. Box 1606
Crosby, Texas 77532
866 241-7510

Edited By
Judy Howell
Crosby, Texas

Cover Photos
Stephens Family, Thompson Family, Lloyd Family, Howell Family,
Coyle Family, Hadaway Family, Vanderhoofven Family, Fyffe Family

Cover Design
Lloyd and Judy Shelby

Photos in Book
Family Albums
Dating Back to 1900

Harvey Thomas Lloyd and Anna Fyffe Lloyd
Wedding Day
February 21, 1924

FOREWORD

Lloyd Shelby is a Texas treasure and if Texas has yet to realize it, one day she soon shall.

I met Lloyd a while back and almost before he opened his mouth you had to figure he's a Texican and you didn't have to talk to him long before your suspicions would be confirmed. In those few moments, as his Texas roots became evident, there could also be no doubt that's just the way he likes it.

He radiates the feeling of personal pride in his family's heritage, those who played many parts in the taming of that great state. On the stage presenting, in a classroom, or at the campfire, he is dynamic in gesture and honest in thought. Combine that spirit with his enjoyment in writing, love of sharing, and willingness to educate those unfamiliar to the many sides of the American Cowboy, then you'll start to understand why I refer to Cowboy Lloyd Shelby as a Texas treasure.

The recollection of a little history, heritage, cowboy lore, and those special folks that help mold his life (both living and dead), bundled around cowboy parables and desires, and you have Lloyd Shelby's latest contribution to the fading art of Cowboy Poetry, the book entitled "I REMEMBER."

Starting off, the cover gives rise to many stories. Photos taken from family albums shows both stern and smiley faces, either by choice or circumstance, as they carved their names in Texas history. Stories shared here with rhyme and rhythm, from the Texas pioneers laboring for a better life to the day-to-day survival of ranch life that'll both toughen and stir the heart.

As the title indicates the theme of the book is "Remembering." Memories drawn from both personal experiences and stories passed down. Asking questions such as "Can we go back once more", and in some cases if we could, is it really where we'd like to stay?

Tales from memories as in "Not Forgotten, "Ol Pop", and "Diamond John Coyle." Editorials as in "Texas Ladies", "River Oaks Honk Tonk", and "Cowboy And The Lawyer". So many others, each to play on the reader's own experiences and memories, each to leave the reader to ponder, "Can we go back once more?"

I am honored to have been the one Lloyd chose to share all these remembrances with first.

Thank you Lloyd,

Mike Dunn   Cowboy Poet   Mesa, Arizona

INTRODUCTION

What is it that comes from deep inside of our souls that compels us to remember? As I visited with a long time friend of mine this morning, Todd Cave, I was amazed at how many times during our conversation he used the phrase, "I remember".

All of us in one way or the other are excited, saddened, frightened or relieved at things that come to us in our memories. Only a select few have the ability to write about their memories and of that select few, a much smaller few have the ability to write their memories in rhyme. Lloyd Shelby is one of those select individuals.

In literature, Cowboy Poetry has become a celebration of many things that we remember. Cowboy Poets remember their history, their family, their friends, their work and their love of God and his creations through their words.

Lloyd's first poem in this book is titled, "I Remember", and it sets the pace and prepares the reader for more memories to come. Each entry in the book is based on a memory and through Lloyd's ability to rhyme; the reader will find themselves caught up in his exciting words.

One of the first poems that reached out and grabbed me was the story of a young cowboy that went to heaven way too soon. It made me remember one of my first poems that related to a similar situation.

From **"Cowboy at Rest"**…….

"Our memories of the one that's gone, hurt yet
   help us heal.
Without our faith in the One above, we wouldn't
   Know what to feel."

Or the poem that tells about the "good ole days" which brings the reader in close contact with the transitions of the life of a cowboy.

From **"Memories"**…….

"The ground was harder than he remembered it, from his
   youth as a young ranch hand.
When he gathered cows and checked the fence and rode
   Across the land."

Or the story of the eternal love of an old cowboy as he shares his reminisces of a life gone by.

From **"Not Forgotten"**….

"I gazed at her there, with smile so fine, and hair like new spun gold.
And wished the moment to last forever, in my memory
   To have and to hold."

Or from the true family story passed down through generation of Diamond John Coyle and how a game of cards changed his life and the lives of those to come. And you must read the poem in its entirety to find out exactly what happened to young John Coyle.

From "**Diamond John Coyle**"......

"From somewhere up north came a young buck, John Coyle was his given name.
He'd come to Texas to make his fortune, and maybe even some fame."

A mystique surrounds cowboy poets, a mystique that gives them a story telling ability that will hold you on the edge of your seats. Lloyd Shelby has this quality and it is emphasized in this wonderful collection of poems.

As Lloyd weaves his words, you the reader will be pulled into the tapestry of his memories. As the tapestry unfolds, you too, will become a part of, "I Remember".

Linda Kirkpatrick   Cowboy Poet
    Author of   "SOMEWHERE IN THE WEST"

Table of Contents

Forword
Preface
Dedication

I Remember	1
Other Side of The Dawn	3
Cowboy At Rest	5
Cowboy's Prayer	7
Memories	9
Not Forgotten	11
Cowboy	12
I Should Have Been Born Rich	13
Diamond John Coyle	15
Big Sky	19
Answered prayer	20
Diamonds and Pearls	23
Family	25
For Love	27
Healing	29
Rabbit Ropin'	31
Jimmie	33
Lone Star Legacy	34
Lost Love	35
My Love	39
Ol Pop	41
Cowboy and the Lawyer	43
Texas Ladies	46
The Journey	47
From The Shadows	48
The Visit	51
River Oaks Honky Tonk	52
Sacrifice	54
Long Road Home	55
The Hand	57
Her Smile	59
Just Call Me "W"	60
The Silver Screen	62
A Wedding Promise	65

Cowbiography

Preface

The ties to our past seem to be a tenuous tie when we are young and often become stronger as we grow older. It was interesting to me when I was young and was dragged to family reunions with my parents, how the "old folks" liked to talk about "the good old days" and just laughed and carried on.

Us kids just did our own fun things, but I used to stop when I got hot and listen. Somewhere along the way I became more interested in our family history and history in general. Mom used to take great pride in showing us kids pictures of great granddad who came to Texas from Tennessee with all the kids and ma. And how, even farther back, we were related to a Cherokee woman who was the first of her gender to sit on the tribal council.

My love for my heritage comes quite naturally, then. I think that as you read this, some of you will realize that you feel the same way.

I have also been deeply touched by my wife's love of family. Her family has always been very close, as evidenced by the story of "Diamond John Coyle", contained in this book. Her mother and father were inseparable from the time they first fell in love, a total of over fifty five years.

As a writer of poetry, I am humbled when I read a poem written in the late fifties or early sixties by my wife's mother, Gladys Thompson, called,

"Compensation"

We were sweethearts, you and I, in time
   long past.
You were young and handsome, when I found love at last.
   Each time I saw you coming, my heart was all aglow.
   I felt I couldn't love you more, how little does youth know.

> *Two score years have passed & now, your hair has turned to gray.*
> *But when I see you coming, my heart glows in a different way.*
> *Young love's a stream dancing gaily, a ripple of constant delight,*
> *While old love's a steady river, that flows with strength and might.*
> *With the passing of youth and its pleasures, many hearts feel love is done.*
> *But old love brings a new beauty, that makes up for not being young.*

Later, this wise and gentle woman wrote one other letter to her husband that should give us all a lesson in living, in love, and in family heritage. This personal letter is shared with the permission of Gladys Thompson's daughter, my wife, Judy.

Dear Charles,

Today is a very special day for me. It's my forty fifth wedding anniversary and I have this to say.

I had a mother and father who really loved each other, so I know what love is. I have seen three teenagers safely through the traumatic teens, so I know what satisfaction is.

I have prayed, and my prayers have been answered, so I know what faith is.

And I've had by my side for forty-five beautiful years, the kindest, gentlest, most considerate human being I've ever known, so I know what happiness is.

And because I've know all these things, I know what wealth is.

> *I love you,*
>
>   *Gladys*

Now, this book of poetry is titled, "I REMEMBER", because it looks at a cowboy's remembrances of his life. I will not be able to duplicate the wonderful expression of memories from the beautiful, "Miss Gladys", so, I'll just take my hat off to all who use their God-given talents to take us back to those times that give us such warm, and lasting memories, whether they use music, art, or the written and spoken word.

They say that, over time, we tend to remember the good times and things, and bad memories gradually fade. That seems to be true, at least from my own experience.

As a writer of things pertaining to cowboys, I find that events that were pretty darned serious at the time they occurred sometimes are quite humorous from the perspective of a few years. That wreck on the horse during branding where I got rolled on by my horse and busted up pretty bad, well, it can make for a real interesting story about how not to get into that type situation! Course, quite a few years had to pass for that to be funny, I can tell you for sure!

But each of us has our own special remembrances of our life that are often triggered by something we see or hear. For me, those memories come flooding back quite regularly, these days. I guess I sort of enjoy re-living those rich times spent with friends and relatives and those beautiful sights, sounds and smells I encountered as I traveled

As we grow older, as we all must do, many times our memories tend to keep us young, at least in heart. Our imaginations are what we actually lose. I hope to never lose that beautiful gift of imagination I often refer to in my performances, for it is freely given to each of us by the Creator, yet it is frequently, subtly stolen, by our fast-paced society.

Like precious jewels kept in a safe and taken out periodically to admire and polish, so are our memories. In this collection of my remembrances, I want to share with you many of the things that have made me who I am, as well as some things that are strictly a part of my imagination. It will be up to you to determine which are memories and which are imagination. Not that it really matters, because we all seem to embellish events, don't we?

I have included pictures for many of the stories in this work. I find that they add to the reader's perception of the story much like the old stereoscope. If a picture is worth a thousand words, then this is, indeed, a very long book!

Some of the pictures are of my family and my wife's family. Others are from museum archives and friends. I guess I could have used some from your family albums, also, but I couldn't reach you in time, or you didn't answer the phone!

The title poem, "I REMEMBER", was written, as many of my works are, on the back of a napkin or paper towel, in a restaurant or bar. "I REMEMBER" was written in Crosby, Texas in Lonestar Catfish and Ribs, owned by two of my good neighbors, Mike and Val. I simply got to "remembering" while waitin' on my catfish, and it just sort of came out. They liked it and I hope you will, too.

If you like this collection of poems and "stories in rhyme", then perhaps you should check into some other cowboy poets. A good resource for this genre is the internet website, "*CowboyPoetry.com*". This website is the largest collection of cowboy poetry, classic and contemporary, on the entire internet and you're bound to find something you like.

Finally, I would encourage you, the reader, to allow yourself the time to remember those wonderful days when you were a kid and your imagination could take you to places and times you so enjoy reading about today. Remember, no one can take your imagination and memories from you, unless you let them do so.

So, listen to your memories. Remember. Savor those sweet times, and enjoy!

As you read "**I Remember**", I hope you find something to trigger some fine old memories from your past. If so, then you may want to open that old vault of you memory and "polish" those old gems.

Just a Ridin',   *Lloyd Shelby*

DEDICATION

This book and its memories are dedicated to my dear wife, Judy, for without her love and encouragement and countless hours of proofing, this and all my other endeavors, would be just scraps of paper in some file. My admiration for her, and her heritage, is expressed in this work, specifically, "My Love" and "Diamond John Coyle". Thanks, JuJu!

Our memories often seem to just naturally flow to those "good times" in the past. Whilst sittin' in **Lone Star Catfish and Ribs** in Crosby, Texas, eatin' the best darned catfish and hush puppies around, I began writin' on a paper towel some of them good times, and this is what came out.

I REMEMBER

I Remember – days that the sun came up slow,
        A warm kiss from my mom,
        With no particular place to go.
        Soft summer rain,
        A cork on an ole cane pole,
        Grasshoppers and lightening bugs,
        Secrets never told.

I Remember – my second grade teacher,
        And the sweet girl in front of me,
        Billy, Steve and Jimmy and our
        famous fort, up in that old oak tree.
        Lemonade so tart, it made your
          mouth pucker,
        Tootsie rolls, moon pies, and those
          gooey all day suckers.
        Church on Sunday mornings,
        Fried chicken with gravy and apple
          pie,
        Laying on your back in the cool
          grass,
        Staring at a deep blue Texas sky.
        Crankin' that ice cream freezer,
        Dominos on the porch,
        Catchin' frogs in the creek,
        As the sun our backs would scorch!

I Remember – that first pony dad gave me,
        When I was only seven.
        It seemed I owned the world,
        I'd died and gone to Heaven!

The day grandma died, why'd she
    have to leave?
T'was the first loss I'd ever seen,
I learned what it meant to grieve.
My first real love, my heart turned
    over hard.
I asked her to be my girl, out in her
    dad's front yard.

I Remember – the day I said "I do",
    My mother's tears, dad's proud
        smile,
    My baby's first new shoes.
    The kid's first grade classes,
    The bus ride to school each day.
    I was so proud at graduation,
    I didn't know what to say.
    My daughter's wedding day,
    The grandkids laugh I hear.
    Memories so vivid,
    In my mind they still are clear.

I Remember – all these things and many,
    many more.
    So much to fill a life up with,
    But now I must close the door.
    For 'tis time to go on home,
    The place I long to be.
    And gaze upon my Master's face,
    The One I've longed to see.

I Remember – He promised to walk this
    journey,
    And go with me all the way.
    So I've enjoyed this ride I've been
    on,
    Now the end of a long, happy day!

It's during those beautiful dreams we have sometimes, that we go places we can't quite remember when we awake, yet they leave us with an indescribable feeling of peace. This is one of those dreams, that came true. That's the way He is!

THE OTHER SIDE OF THE DAWN

He'd gone to sleep late that night, after the
   midnight watch was over.
The campfire had burned down low, he was one
   real tired drover.
But when he woke he felt refreshed, like he'd
   never felt before.
The sun was bright but not too hot, his body
   wasn't sore.
The sounds around the chuckwagon, were
   somehow different, too.
The smell of the coffee and bisquits and beans, he
   didn't have a clue,
As to what was goin' on, he didn't recognize this
   place.
The wonder and puzzlement, registered on his
   face.
Now this old buckaroo had seen some places,
   that'd set your mind on end.
There was Wyomin', and the Montana sky, and
   the land around Big Bend.
But this here place was marvelous, awesome
   beyond compare!
He may have dreamed about it once, a place so
   fine and fair.
The trees all had perfect shape, the grass so long
   and green,
The creeks were full of clear water and fish, the
   cattle the best he'd seen.
He no longer was hot and dusty, but felt all fresh
   and new.
His clothes were comfortable beyond compare,
   the sky a crystal blue.

And then the Head Wrangler was there, to show him round the place,
He was a tall buckaroo, with light shinin' from his face.
He told him he was finally home, his ridin' days were through,
He'd had his last roundup, but he'd have other things to do.
Now his job was to sing and tell, stories to one and all,
About those days when he'd first heard, that first low cattle call.
And how'd he'd tended the herd's down there, and helped keep them on the trail,
The men he'd known, the songs he'd sung, and many a cowboy tale.
Then he finally realized, this was the place of which he'd always heard,
A place called the "sweet by and by", with nary a discouraging word.
So the words and music together, told the story in a sweet, sweet song,
As this cowboy reached his final home, the other side of the dawn.

In June of 2002, a dear family of friends of mine lost their son. I hurt with them, even though I never knew Colby. Yet, I knew them and the love that guided them in all they do. I wrote what my heart told me to put on paper and sent it to them during their time of mourning. When I saw them again in Luckenbach, Texas, I asked for their permission to use this poem, as a tribute to Colby. They only said, "Of course, he would have loved it". Here's to you, cowboy.

COWBOY AT REST

A cowboy went home the other day, he was ours,
   but he was yours, too.
You see he was the one we loved, they'll be a lot
   of healing to do.

When a loved one is gone too soon, we often
   question why.
There has to be an answer out there, as we stare
   up at the sky.

Our memories of the one that's gone, hurt, yet
   help us heal.
Without our faith in the One above, we wouldn't
   know what to feel.

A single star in the heavens at night, we know to
   be a friend,
Who's there to help our cowboy son, show that
   this is not the end,

But rather, just a part of our journey, that we all
   must travel on.
Cause we'll all see each other again, when we go
   beyond the dawn.

So our cowboy is up there now, "keepin' that fire
 a burnin',
Yes, he's missed down here, for him our hearts
 are yearnin'

But we'll see him soon enough, but we still got
 work here to do,
Tellin' others the Good News of Him, and that He
 cares for you!

So we keep on travellin' day by day, you're in our
 hearts, cowboy son,
We'll see you by the campfire up there, when our
 work down here is done.

To Colby

There aren't many cowboys who are atheists. Time spent working in God's creation just naturally leads one to understand that there is an order to this ole world. While working on a ranch in Mertzon, Texas, I had an encounter with the "Sky Guy". This was how I expressed that time spent with Him.

A COWBOY'S PRAYER

A cowboy rode alone one day, roundin' up some strays,
When he paused atop a gentle rise, where he could see for quite ways.

There was hills and valleys, and trees and clouds, as far as the eye could see.
And he began to quietly contemplate, just how this came to be.

It didn't look like no accident, like some folks tried to teach.
To think that would take believin', against what his mom had always preached!

So he listened to the gentle wind, that rustled through the trees,
And watched a deer go runnin' by, as pretty as you please.

He marveled at the hawk up high, a ridin' on the air.
Removin' his hat, he bowed his head, and spoke this simple prayer:

"Sir, I don't know much about, how this ol' world came to be,
I just know you seem to care, for cowboys just like me."

"So thank you, Sir, for givin' me, a place to work and ride,
Where I can see your handiwork, with you right by my side."

"And thank you for that simple book, that tells us of your Son,
You must be really proud of Him, and what He went and done."

"I'm really proud and humbled, 'bout what your Book does say,
'Bout how I can also be your son, cause yours showed us the way."

I know how much you love this place, I really love it, too.
So I'll do my best to care for it, in everything I do."

"Thanks is not near enough, to say how I truly feel.
But I know you can see my heart, and know my words is real."

"I gotta go now, Sir, and finish out my day.
Thanks again for all you've done, and givin' me my say!"

While contemplating the journey one day, my mind began to remember the "good ole days". And while some cowboys like to have you believe there's nothing as good as sleeping outdoors, on the ground, they often forget the cold, rain, mud, snow, and how really hard it is. But our memories are that way.

MEMORIES

The ground was harder than he remembered it, from his
    youth as a young ranch hand.
When he gathered cows and checked the fence and rode
    across the land.

Yes, the years had seemed to rush on by, now he really
    felt them, too.
His cowboyin' years were part of his past, he'd chosen
    other things to do.

Now he rode a car to work each day, steel and glass
    canyons boxed him in.
But the creases on his face he'd earned, a reminder of
    where he'd been.

As he looked out the cool glass window, of this building
    so tall and high,
He remembered those days of his ramblin' youth, with
    nothin' above but sky.

And the thought had crossed his busy mind, could he go
    back just once again?
To feel those wide open spaces, far from the cities loud
    din.

So he'd made a quick decision, an escape for a day or
    two.
No need to change his mind now, it was the right thing
    to do.

So he gathered up his 'roll, his jeans, and spurs and
 boots and hat,
And headed for the country, where his heart was really
 at.

And renewed a long lost friendship, a rancher friend of
 old.
They exchanged many fond memories, when both were
 young and bold.

He rode across the rancher's land, the memories flooded
 back, so strong.
The sights, the smells, the grass and trees, where th wind
 played her own sweet song.

That night he made his camp, beneath an old oak tree,
And decided he'd really missed all this, 'twas here that
 he should be.

As he closed his eyes that night, his mind tried to find a
 way,
That he could come back out here, to work and live and
 stay.

But he knew it was only a pipe-dream, somethin' he'd
 never do,
So he went on off to sleep, where his memories, at least,
 were true.

And when he woke in the mornin', the ground was hard
 and cold.
His body was sure achin', and remindin' him he was
 getting' old.

So he said adios to his pardner, the rancher, his friend to
 this day.
But that night on the ground had convinced him, a soft
 bed was where he wanted to stay!

Sometimes, the things we don't say, say more than any words. This story is a long one, but short in words.

NOT FORGOTTEN

The afternoon sun was warm and bright, as we sat underneath that old tree.
We'd ridden the buggy out from town, my dog, my sweetheart and me.

The blanket was spread out in the shade, a lunch of chicken, biscuits and tea.
We were ready to relax away the day, my dog, my sweetheart, and me.

I gazed at her there, with smile so fine, and hair like new spun gold.
And wished the moment to last forever, in my memory to have and to hold.

But I suddenly woke up and found, myself at the graveside to be.
And remembered that time long ago, with my dog, my sweetheart, and me.

I remember many days, just like this one. Seems a cowboy is blessed thata way.

COWBOY

The hawk circles aimlessly, lookin' for her prey,
He stares over the hot, dry land, facin' another long, hard day.

It is, indeed, a lonely job, in a line shack huntin' strays,
Especially in country rough as this, a few take several days.

But he loves his job, cowboy his title, proud.
You'll seldom see his type, in the spotlight or in a crowd.

But many there are who'd like to say, they are cowboys, too.
But get them on a horse with a rope, and they haven't got a clue,

To what it takes, from deep inside, that makes a cowboy go.
It has nothin' to do with money or fame, or bein' head of the show.

No, it's a love for God's Creation, and the creatures placed in his care,
That keeps him doin' his job everyday, when no one for miles is near.

So, the hawk circles aimlessly, lookin' for her prey,
And he stares over the hot, dry land, facin' another day.

My mother likes this because it allows her to tell folks she would have settled for just one of the two! Oh, mom, give me a break!

I SHOULD HAVE BEEN BORN RICH
(INSTEAD OF JUST GOOD LOOKIN')

My mother always loved me, at least that's what she
   always said,
I believe she really meant it, as she tucked me in my bed.

Dad was a little more quite, about the way he felt.
You see, he was the one who encouraged me, (when
   needed it),…with the back side of his belt!

My dog was reluctant at first, to follow me around,
Until mom had me drag those pork chops, behind me on
   the ground.

The girls in school liked the football players, and all
   those other jocks,
Who wore those real cool uniforms, but had those smelly
   socks!

But this cowboy wasn't cool back then, like he is today.
I was the "strong silent type", who didn't have much to
   say.

But folks today say I've changed since then, no longer
   near as quite.
I've spoken in some places where, we almost had a riot!

Complainin' didn't seem to help at all, about my looks
   I'm talkin'.
The girls saw me in the hall, and keep right on a walkin'.

But I got con-fi-dence, about the way I look,
I learned to accept my handsome-ness, I learned it from
   a book!

But money's always been pretty scarce, my wallet way too thin.
Been caught payin' for a meal at lunch, with only a silly grin.

And I left real quick in my pickup truck, down that road 'a hookin',
And wished that I'd been born rich……
(instead of just good lookin'!)

Stories of fortunes won, and lost, on the turn of a card, are numerous in our western heritage. Early in the last century, a young man came to Texas in search of that often elusive dream of fame and fortune. This is a true story of how he fared, as told by his granddaughter, Ms. Judy Hadaway of Gladewater, Texas, now my wife.

DIAMOND JOHN COYLE

The light was bright in the dimly lit room, oer' the table
  where the game was goin' on.
Chips and money and cards were scattered, in front of
  the players, every one.

The game had been one of those long affairs, that lasted
  for days and days,
With some comin and playin' awhile, till their minds
  went into a haze.

Another would come and take the place, of the fallen
  comrade in arms,
And hope ol' Lady Luck would visit, and grace him with
  her charms.

Ft. Worth was still a rowdy cow town, in 1922,
With cowboys and cattlemen and oilmen there, lookin'
  for something to do.

From somewhere up north came a young buck, John
  Coyle was his given name.
He'd come to Texas to make his fortune, and maybe
  even some fame.

The stockyard was still a rough place back then, for a
  young man to learn how to live.
Few mistakes were tolerated here, fewer still knew how
  to forgive.

John had a hard earned hundred dollars, to help him get
 started out.
But he was a man of destiny, of that there can be no
 doubt.

He was drawn to the game, like a moth to a flame, By
 the lights in the "Elephant" that night.
The cards and the chips - of red and blue, was a mighty
 powerful sight.

Especially to a young man, with destiny a part of his
 name.
The town didn't know of him yet, but that was about to
 change!

He watched from the side of the room, as the game kept
 grindin' on.
Poker could be a wicked mistress, who sang a sirens
 song.

Johnny decided to take a chance, when a chair finally
 opened up.
The old timers laughed and spit and cursed, who was
 this here young pup?

They laughed at his hundred dollar stake, he'd be an
 easy one to pick clean.
Why, he was one of them "Yankee Boys", many of them
 they had seen.

But something they missed in this man, would change
 them all this night.
Each would learn not to judge a book by the cover, or a
 man just at first sight.

The game started slow, five dollars a hand at first,
And Johnny won most of those pots, his luck better,
 theirs now the worse.

The stakes began to get bigger, to frighten this young
one away.
But the "Lady" was perched firm on his shoulder, t'was
here she wanted to stay.

Some sweated and cursed their luck that night, another
folded and left his chair.
That one put his hands on his face, shook his head while
his eyes just stared.

For Johnny was in charge of the table now, no one was
arguing that.
Except for the cattleman across from him, with red
bandana and high creased hat.

The stakes were mighty high by now, piled up on that
table green,
It was the most money bet on poker, that any had ever
seen.

Johnny was bluffin', the cowman said, he could feel it in
his bones that night.
He'd bet the last thing that he had, a diamond ring
sparklin' bright.

A hush fell over the place, as the final call was made.
Each had only the cards in his hand, the devil had to be
paid.

The cowman had a grin on his face, as he laid his cards
on the table.
"Try and beat my two pair young friend, aces high, if
you think that you're able".

Johnny simply stared at the cards, with no look anyone
there could read.
Was he happy or sad or what, was there something in his
eyes like greed?

Everyone was now holdin' their breath, for the moment
   of truth had come.
Johnny slowly laid down his cards, but he did it one by
   one.

One lady, a queen, showed her royal face, a sister soon
   joined her there.
If the next one was a Jack or an Ace, all he might have
   was two pair.

But the third card, too, was a lady, real royaly now
   gracin' the table.
Did young Johnny have their sister they thought ? If he
   didn't, his "Lady" was certainly able!

Like in slow motion, he threw the last one down, to join
   her sisters there.
Four of a kind could always beat, aces high, two pair.

The money helped young John Coyle, get a start in
   Texas back then.
But that beautiful shiny diamond ring, is what put on his
   face a grin.

Cause that sweet young lady he'd met,
   named Millie had stolen his heart.
And now that diamond sealed his fate, for
   those two would never part.

And now that ring is worn upon my hand,
   from my grandmother to my mom, you see.
Mine now to pass on to mine, our granddad
   John's Legacy.

BIG SKY

The air was crisp and clear, on the mountain side that
   night.
Cattle all was restin' easy, the sky a sparklin' bright.

It seemed he could see for miles and miles, across the
   celestial quilt.
And he just kinda marveled at, the beauty God had built.

There musta been a million stars, or maybe even more.
He couldn't remember seein' so many, at any time
   before.

And those Northern Lights a dancin', the colors beyond
   compare.
He wished he could capture them, with his sweetheart
   them to share.

But he had a deep down peace inside, that only He can
   give.
That makes the journey easier, as each day he would
   live.

So he said a simple prayer, thankin' the Boss and not
   askin' why,
And went to sleep there by the fire, beneath God's big,
   Big Sky.

Many of us turn to prayer in our time of need, but often it is as a last resort. That seems to be human nature. However, sometimes the answer is much different than we could ever imagine! Here is a case in point, from a time in our past, that should not amaze you, if you truly believe!

ANSWERED PRAYER

They waited in the shallow place, upon the open plain.
Guns loaded and ready for the charge, it just seemed insane.

Twenty men dressed in blue, from the fort now far away.
Facing these Comanches three hundred strong, the devil would get his pay.

The sun was ridin' low in the west, behind the Comanches there.
Each soldier resigned to his fate, they'd all now turned to prayer.

A whoop was raised from three hundred throats, as the charge was to begin.
And the thundering horde descended upon, these twenty blue clad men.

Each said a final prayer and clenched his gun real tight.
For what was going to happen next, wouldn't be a pretty sight!

The Indians were almost upon them, when they stopped with eyes open wide,
And dropped their bows and lances, on the ground to either side.

Now nothing scares a Comanche brave, except something from the great unknown.
For everything could be conquered by gun or bow, or a lance rightly thrown.

But these braves turned their ponies quick, and headed
back to the west.
The soldiers couldn't believe their eyes, what had
happened? ......unless,

They slowly turned around to see, what was behind them
there,
And saw what had scared the Comanche braves, an
answer to all their prayers.

For there stood twenty of the biggest men, that they had
ever seen.
Each was over ten feet tall, their skin with a deep bronze
gleam.

Light shone from their hair, a giant sword was in one
hand.
Their robes were white as the winter snow, spread over
the desert sand.

But it was the fire in their eyes, that was bright as the
noonday sun,
That had made those fearsome Comanches turn tail, and
from that spot to run.

The men in blue fell to their knees, for the sight was
awesome to behold.
They were God's own angels true, of them they'd all
been told.

Then they heard a booming voice, that was somehow
soft and low.
Which spoke to each soldier there, of the path they were
to go.

And when each could finally look up, the angels were no
longer there.
But the time spent down upon their knees, took away all
their care.

They mounted up and headed back, to the fort so far
away.
Each trying to figure out, the meaning of this day.

And the Comanche tribes still talk about, the battle on
that day.
About the mighty "soldiers" seen, but words would
never say,

Of how those Comanche braves, had seen the Great
Spirit's face,
And caused them to turn and run, from that "holy" place.

So the blue clad men and Comanche, in skin of deepest
red,
Went back to their own tribes, but it has oft been said,

That we are all protected by angels, who usually go
unseen.
But sometimes He will show them to us, new faith to all
to bring!

I think this ole cowboy may just have figured it all out! I know you gals will probably agree.

DIAMONDS AND PEARLS

He'd been workin' on the ranch, for more years than most folks knew.
'Cause it was the kind of work he liked, the "natural" thing to do.

He came to town on occasion, for a beer and pool and to dance.
But he'd pretty much given up, on findin' real romance.

For sure he'd loved a gal one time, or two, but then who's countin'.
But findin' that one, real love, was harder than climbin' a mountain.

But one day as he was buyin', a tractor for the chores to do.
He met a perfect stranger, with eyes like the sky, so blue.

And he paused to look her over, a beauty she surely was.
Her eyes had captured his heart, and his head was all a buzz.

He remained calm on the outside, but his gizzard was a twitchin'.
The only thing close to it, was a bucking horse, a pitchin'!

He knew it then, was certain, for true, that this gal was all he needed.
But how could he be so fortunate? His heart with his mind, it pleaded.

They talked and looked at each other, for hours and days and days.
When they both realized, they'd made it through the haze.

He was hard-headed, known by all to be like nails, so hard,
But fair in all his dealin's, easy to call a "pard".

But just like a raw diamond, he needed polishin' and fixin', for sure.
Cause on the outside he wasn't flashy, but inside he was pure.

She was really pretty, a sparkle in her eye.
I've already told of her beauty, how it rivals the Texas sky.

But she was more like a precious pearl, that comes from the oceans deep.
Which shines with iridescence, so delicate, you'd have to weep.

And like a beautiful necklace, they were always meant to be.
Diamonds and Pearls together, a beautiful sight to see!

Those who are adopted by someone, whether as a baby, or as an adult, know exactly what this is about.

FAMILY

Time was, blood was thicker than thin, and family would
    stick together.
No matter what adversity, they'd go through any
    weather.

But "family" is a deeper thing, much more than closest
    kin.
It belongs to those who make a choice, that comes from
    deep within.

Cause there are those from far and wide, with no blood
    kin are they blessed.
But often they've found "family", who turn out to be the
    best.

It seems some folks have real big hearts, that never get
    full at all.
They seem to have love enough, when they hear a lonely
    heart call,

From someone who has lost their way, or been left out in
    the cold.
They'll always be a place for them, whether young or
    very old.

So you that are truly blessed, with blood kin who love
    you now,
Remember there are others who, take love and show us
    how,

That God really intended for, His family to be comprised.
So open up your inner love, and you may be surprised,

At how marvelous a family can be, when we love unselfishly.
And become a part of the best, God's big, big family.

11/2/98

Some love stories are beautiful, some are funny, and some are both at the same time. This is one of those that will definitely bring tears to your eyes.

FOR LOVE

This is the tale of a lake found in Texas, and how it got
  it's name.
And at the end of the lovers tale, you'll understand it's
  fame.

T'was before the time of the white man, two tribes had
  been at war,
For such a very long time, no one could remember what
  for.

But each had settled on the shores, of a lake that was
  long, but not wide.
A natural barrier between the two, each on the opposite
  side.

So a sort of easy peace was found, and lasted for many a
  moon.
But all that was destined to change, and it would happen
  soon.

Spring was now finally come, like roses on the new vine.
And a boy's fancy turns, you know, to things of the
  feminine kind.

A young maiden was at the shore one day, getting water
  for a meal,
When a glance across the lake stopped her there, her fate
  this look would seal.

The young warrior was leading his ponies, to a drink at
  the lake's far shore.
And his gaze met that of the maiden. He knew it would
  lead to more.

Love was in their eyes and hearts, it wasn't very hard to see,
Each longed for the other's embrace, this was certainly meant to be.

Each day they came down to the shore, the deep love shown in their eyes.
Like the sun on a cool, crisp morning fair, They both pledged their lives.

Spring now turned into summer, finally summer into the fall.
And on opposite sides they gazed each day, both giving it their all.

Then on one clean, cold morning, He no longer could hold it back,
And eagerly leaped into the lake. In courage, he did not lack.

He was young and strong and in love, so he swam toward the opposite shore.
But the water was, oh, so very cold, Could he possibly give it any more?

The answer was finally beginning to show, his strength was now almost gone.
And just shy of his true love's embrace he sank, the end of this warrior's song.

Each tribe had seen the drama unfold, they were quite when it came to an end.
No emotion was shown as they went to their camps. What message was this to send?

But both tribes came together that day, to make peace and pay homage to cupid.
And they named that lake after that young warrior's quest, for they named it……….**"Lake Stupid"**!

Cowboys often don't let their feelings show. Maybe they should. But we all must listen to this story's message, in order to be free enough to "let it go, and live"!

HEALING

Some bruises never show, on the outside where people see.
They're on the heart and soul, deeper than is believed.

Some are caused by people, without knowing what they have done.
Others are intentional, by the devils own daughter or son.

But some are self inflicted, by our own minds not letting go,
Of words we have misunderstood, or actions from long ago.

These deep hurts may not heal, they follow you everywhere.
So no one else can help, you think, there's no way to repair.

But we do have a choice, if to our spirit we will listen,
A way to break the chains and escape, from this terrible, mental prison.

Whether you believe in Him or not, you should at least Consider,
Is it better to finally heal and leave, or let your life remain bitter?

His voice will not be loud and big, like some people that we have heard.
His still, small voice you will hear, and He'll speak those comforting Words,

That will sooth and begin to take away the pain, and heal
your heart and soul.
To teach you about forgiveness, and make you, once
again, whole.

Turn your heart toward Jesus, He understands your hurts
and fears.
He'll give you a brand new heart, and wipe away your
tears.

Cause He suffered for you and me, and knows about all
the pain.
Your mind will finally be free, and heaven you'll have
gained.

But it will be here and now, not years and years to come.
Trust in Him and Him alone, for He is God's own Son!

This ain't no joke. I have seen some buckaroos do some pretty strange things when out alone. My pardner, "Cactus Jack" Gildersleave didn't know I was watchin' him on the Blue Rock pasture, but I swear I nearly fell off my horse laughing as I was watchin' that nut try and rope two or three of those West Texas Jack Rabbits. Fact is, it was from that episode that Jack and I founded the AJRHA, the American Jack Rabbit Horse Association, discussed in another of my previous works.

RABBIT ROPIN'

Now it may strange, when you're talkin' 'bout ropin',
To mention rabbits, sets your mind to hopin',

That this ole cowboy, ain't lost his mind.
Cause if he has , he's not the kind,

To get to tellin' 'bout somethin' new, unless he's done it,
Or knows someone who,

Has taken a rope and thrown a loop, at a jack rabbit runnin' free,
It seems them things are so darn quick, you wind up ropin' a tree.

'Cause them ole jacks are quick to move, and duck and twist and turn.
Then you'll finally realize, you got a lot to learn.

This ain't a calf that runs real straight, nor a steer who's big and lean,
A jack rabbit don't like a horse. on ropes he ain't real keen.

He just wants to run in Texas,and other parts around.
Don't need a lot for happiness, just sky and brush and ground.

So why do these crazy cowboys, keep comin' after
   him so much.
If they want to get a rabbit, go get one from a hutch!

So when you think you how to rope, a goat, calf, steer,
   or cow.
I'm dyin' if I'm lyin', you really don't know how!

Friends often don't know how much they affect us, just by being themselves.

JIMMIE

You make my day much brighter, when the sun refuses
   to shine,
And help me see more beauty, in this cowboy life of
   mine.

Your laughter is sweet medicine, that soothes my
   anxiety.
I know you don't believe it, but you are a real blessing to
   me.

I love to see the twinkle , in your eyes when you're
   feeling good.
Or when you've stretched the truth, a little more than
   you should.

Your hair makes me breathless, it's as fine as new spun
   gold.
With a trace of another color, which you say, makes you
   feel old.

But you, dear Jimmie, are ageless, you'll always be the
   best.
Especially to this ole cowboy, with you as my friend,

I Am Blessed!

Texas is as much a part of me as life. With Davy Crockett as an ancestor, I have an extra love for what Texas is. This was written for the San Jacinto Day festivities in 2001, held at the place where Texas won her Independence from Mexico, in April, 1836.

LONE STAR LEGACY

No sound of battle, is now heard o'er our land,
From San Jacinto, Goliad, or the Alamo's last stand.

The cannon are silent, the heroes long gone,
They are the stuff of legends, and many a song.

But we still remember, the final outcome here fought,
And with blood sweat and tears, Ole Texas was bought.

Texas, our dear Texas, so grand and so free,
They fought and won here, yes the future they did see.

For our men and our women, still carry the dream,
Of wide open spaces, the mesquite and the streams.

Of cowboys and Indians, and cattle and oil.
Spaceships and computers, and rich Texas soil.

Yes, the cannon and musket, are no longer needed.
But we must still serve Texas, and their sacrifice heeded.

So, thank you General Sam, Crockett, Travis, and all the others,
We stand here today, your spiritual brothers.

Those who know me and my work, know I love a good Louis L'Amour novel. While I do not pretend to be a Louis L'Amour, I do enjoy a good cowboy hero. This is a story along those lines.

LOST LOVE

He walked into the bar, hat slouched down on his head,
But the look in his eyes spoke volumes, yet left much more unsaid.

He stood alone at the end of the bar, his eyes as cold as ice.
Kinda reminded you of an open grave, or snake eyes on a dice.

There wasn't a lot goin' on, only a few in the place.
No one wanted to speak to him, when they saw the look on his face.

The day has started out bad, awakened by his dreams,
Haunted by the one he'd lost, years ago, it seems.

She had taken away his heart, and body, soul and all.
They were to have been wedded soon, he'd heard that siren's call.

But a bunch of rowdy cowboy's, had come to town one night.
Spoiling for a bunch of hell, lookin' for a fight.

And as they shot their pistols, before the night got started,
One bullet found the heart he loved, and that night she departed.

So now he was dead inside, his heartbeat incidental.
As he waited for the pain to end, the hatred began to kindle.

Those cowboys would be made to pay, for takin' away his love.
They would be judged here first, then face it up above.

Tonight they were comin' back, he'd heard it from a friend.
One way or another, tonight would be the end,

To all those nights alone, without sleep or any rest.
He would soon join his love, somewhere in the west.

He heard them enter town, the hoof beats and their shoutin', loud.
He was able to hear their sound, above the barroom crowd.

They really had no idea, he was lookin' for them tonight.
But the set of his jaw and the hatred was not a pretty sight.

As they entered the place, he shot at them a glance.
He was outnumbered by five to one, he didn't have a chance.

But that didn't seem to bother him, he really didn't care.
So he turned from the bar and faced the room, at the cowboys began to stare.

No one noticed at first, but one did, then two, then more.
But everyone thought nothing of it, as he headed for the door.

Although it was hot outside, he closed and locked the doors real loud.
That was a strange thing to do, he got the attention of the crowd.

"What the hell's the matter with you", one of the cowboys said?
But when they looked at him, his eyes showed he was already dead.

The cowboy's tried to snicker, then their blood ran cold.
His eyes had narrowed and focused, in them their fate was told.

The fear was as thick as mud, the cowboy's hands did shake.
As they glanced at each other, a deal with the devil to make.

The next moment would be remembered, by those who saw the sight,
The whole thing was in slow motion, a classic saloon gun fight.

He drew his gun and fired once, then twice before the others could draw,
No one could remember anyone so fast, he was the best they ever saw.

Another shot was fired, when the two still alive took aim.
One struck him in the shoulder, from the other he saw the flame.

But the shot would miss its target, as he fell over to one side.
His next shot hit the cowboy, and laid him open wide.

Now it was one on one, they both stood and faced each other.
He stared and saw the others face, was this his little brother?

Beneath the slouched hat was a boy so young, he couldn't yet shave his face,
What was he doin' here, in this hell hole of a place?

The kid was uncertain, of what he was gonna do.
But the decision was made for him, as his brother his own gun drew.

He felt the bullet in his chest, he was goin' home at last.
He'd now be with his one true love, this fate for which he'd asked.

The smoke seemed to linger, in the bar room late that night,
The results of the anger there, were not a pretty sight.

But a different picture now shown bright, in the heavens far above,
As he again was united with, his sweetheart, his one true love.

This is from an old cowboy to his new wife, written Christmas Eve 2002.

MY LOVE

I awoke so very early, and with my wife so near.
The smell of her hair, her warm embrace, her breathing I
   could hear.

And I thought how much she means to me, my heart
   began to stir,
And the words flooded into my mind, every one was
   about her.

Of how before her I was alive, but didn't know how to
   live,
As her love became so real to me, it she did freely give.

And the sparkle in her does light, a fire down in my soul.
Making this cowboy feel four square, he's finally been
   made whole.

How she supports the crazy things I do, and listens to my
   hurts,
And take my silly moods in stride, and washes my dirty
   shirts.

But there are things that bother me still, from my past so
   long and hard.
Yet she accepts me as I am, and keeps me as her pard.

She teaches me more every day, about how to love and
   live,
And share with others unselfishly, our love to freely
   give.

So with these feeble words I try to say, what she truly means to me.
I guess it will take many years to come, and then she will finally see,

That she has become my heart, my breath, my right arm, my eyes, my life.
And I know why God gave her to me, my precious love, my wife.

My granddad raised me during my early years. He, along with my mom, instilled in me the love for Texas and the cowboy way. I still have regular talks with him, though he's been gone for many years. I still miss him a lot.

OL POP

I followed him most all my life, t'was the natural thing
    to do.
"Ol Pop" was my hero then, and my teacher as I grew.

He was respected by other men, they knew he was his
    word.
And he could always be counted on, from others I had
    heard,

How he had been a Ranger, Texas' best, a man to fear.
But I was never afraid of him, as he held me so very
    near.

His shirt was always buttoned up, the collar crisp and
    straight.
"I gotta represent Ol Texas", he said, "That's my destiny,
    my fate".

And I often say his eyes well up, when talkin' bout the
    Alamo.
He wondered about those brave men, and their sacrifice
    not that long ago.

The way he looked at grandma, he smiled when she
    walked by.
He said he really loved that girl, when she passed, I saw
    him cry.

The things he freely gave to me, can't be measured, by scales of men.
And every time I think of him, I remember where we'd been.

Life's journey never has an ending, it's carried by these like me,
Who remember their "Ol Pop", too, and the timeless memories.

Down here in Texas, we love our lawyers, just like everybody loves 'em ! In fact, we've passed a law that they must be buried twenty feet deep, cause deep, deep down, they're really pretty good folks !

This here story has a logical ending, so, if you're a lawyer and don't get it, email me ! I'll send you a diagram.

COWBOY AND THE LAWYER

They eyed each other carefully, across the table , sittin'.
The lawyer primped and clean,…….

the cowboy calm and spittin'.

Each sized up the other, like a hunter watchin' its prey.
Thinkin' a way ahead, what would the other one say?

The lawyer was the first to speak, his words he was
   careful to pick,
'Cause that cowboy across from him, from the country,
   but weren't no hick.
"I hear you know how to rope and ride , steer and bull
   and horse.
So the question I will pose to you, is one you know, of
   course.
"You see, I've heard a cowboy, speaks a language all his
   own.
Comprised of truth and fancy, and piles of bullshit
   thrown".

"So speakin' as a lawyer, one trained in words and
   things legal.
I'd like to know the origin of, the term, Legal Beagle."

Well now, the cowboy looked at him, a thought on his
   mind did cross.
If this lawyer wanted answers, the bull he would surely
   toss.
He spoke real slow, and with a drawl, his words he was
   careful pickin',
This here lawyer man was slick, but needed a lesson, a
   stickin'.
"The term you mention is one well used, by folks both
   far and near.
So it'll come as no surprise to you, it's origin is from
   right here."
"There once was a cowboy, and his dog, so faithful and
   true,
That he named him a name, that said exactly what he
   could do."
"'Cause the little SOB was smarter, than most men he
   had seen.
And for a dog, was ready, by the public, to be seen."

"You see, his real talent was on things, by most,
   considered legal.
'Cause he could always smell a lie, and still remain true
   as a beagle".
"For years he helped decide, cases in court with a judge.
And one thing you could surely count, was, on the truth,
   not to fudge."
"Cause this was one "attorney", though canine, he was
   true,
To a much higher justice, one thing he'd always do".

"And that one thing was special, I'll tell you, just don't
   beg.
He could tell if a lawyer was lyin', and on him, he'd lift
   a leg!"

"So there is where the term was penned, about the dog
   who'd gone legal.
And folks for miles around called him, a true,
   "Legal Beagle."
Well, the cowboy had finally finished, the lawyer didn't
   know what to do.
'Cause the story was a darn good one. but could it be
   really true?
So the lawyer speaks to the cowboy, not sure of how to
   say,
He really liked the tale he'd heard, but his head wasn't
   full of hay!
"What evidence is there, to this tale I've heard today?
   Something that can validate, some proof, you might
say?"

"Well", drawled the cowboy, "I'd tell the truth if'n I was
   you.
"Cause if you try and even stretch the truth, I've told you
   what he'd do."
"And if you look over yonder, in the corner for quite
   awhile,
Sits that one "Legal Beagle", and just guess why he has
   a smile!"

This is one of those pitfalls every cowboy runs into, often over and over again…..intentionally! Texas ladies just have that effect on 'ya!

TEXAS LADIES

Whether young or old, or somewhere in between.
Texas ladies are the best, this cowboy's ever seen.

They come in many flavors, and all are sweet as can be.
Havin' to choose only one, is a choice not left to me!

Known for all their beauty, on the outside most often seen.
But inside just as pretty, as any place you've ever been.

Some work as models or nurses, or mothers or rancher's wives.
But each tries their very best, to lead up-standing lives.

Now I'm sure there are other places, with pretty ladies, too.
But Texas ladies are the best. prob'ly from those skies, so blue!

But there is one who stole my heart, from the moment we first met.
Although so small and petite, she's the best one yet.

Britanny is her sweet name, it was made for her, for true.
This little Texas lady, always has a lot to do.

A smile that's so infectious, with eyes so deep and green.
You, too, will fall in love, with this little Texas Dream!

So my hat's in my hand, every time a Texas Lady I pass.
But my heart remains all tied up, with this tiny Texas Lass.

Reflection, the kind you sometimes do when you have a lucid moment, can be quite interesting.

THE JOURNEY

There comes a time to everyone, especially when you've
  had much to drink,
That things what never made sense, begin to make you
  think.

So what is this thing all about, this journey of years and
  years?
I'm sure it will make a lot more sense, when I've had a
  few more beers.

The journey will continue, with you holdin' on real tight.
And when the end reaches you, you can say you fought
  the fight.

But don't step on the poor and helpless, and make their
  load the worse,
'Cause you who are the stronger, can, on yourself, bring
  a curse.

So thank the One who made you, that you are blessed
  and free,
And let the journey continue, the end will set you free!

FROM THE SHADOWS

I sat beside the campfire, my pipe a quite glow.
And thought of friends and good times had,
   so very long ago.

My mind began to wander, as I watched the smoke spiral
   and swirl.
Thoughts of long rides and lonely nights, and a pretty
   gold haired girl.

Then out of the firelight's dim light, a shadow suddenly
   appeared,
And sat down right across from me, my heart stopped,
   I was a-feared.

I couldn't see a face, for a shadow has none to see.
Yet something was familiar here, who could this
   apparition be?

My mind must be playing games with me, for I thought
   I heard it speak.
But there was no sound from the shadow there, my heart
   was growing weak.

There, again I heard it, just the same as before.
Except this time I understood, the shadow would tell
   me more.

It spoke of times long ago, out in the vast, western land.
Of pioneer families, cowboys and travelers, and soldiers
   buried in the sand.

Of towns that rose and fell, and men's fortunes lost and
   won.
How others fought the good fight, raising families to
   carry on.

Then the shadow grew silent, no word came to my ear.
Yet it remained there near the fire, and others began
   to appear.

Together they sat around me, yet I now felt no fear.
What was going on? Again, I began to hear.

They each spoke, yet as one, together, the tale ebbed and flowed.
And as the words came together, their eyes in the campfire glowed.

Now, this really surprised me, for I thought they would soon disappear.
But the night was gettin' interesting, as these apparitions grew near.

They spoke of how they saw the land, as a sacred gift for all of man.
And how we were now ruining it, and violating the sacred plan.

Then the shadows turned as one, toward the place where I sat,
And waited for me to answer them, I slowly removed my hat,

And let the smoke spiral and swirl, as when the shadow first I saw.
My mind was cogitating a mite, all my nerves was raw.

I didn't have to say a word, they knew my thoughts, I felt.
So I let them know I understood, as on the ground I knelt,

And took some ground into my hand, and let it fall away.
I promised I would protect this earth, for the rest of my natural days.

The shadows all let me know, I was someone they
 would trust,
To follow through on my words, till I, too, joined the
 dust.

Then they simply disappeared, into the campfire's glow.
And my pipe smoke continued to spiral and swirl,
 upward, oh so slow.

And next mornin's light had a special –ness, I hadn't
 seen before,
Like God had closed one path, and opened up a door.

And I rode on down my trail that day, a peace deep in
 my soul,
For now I knew my place down here, a cowboy made
 fully whole!

Love endures. We've all heard that old saying, yet, do we really understand it? Here is a story of someone who truly did.

THE VISIT

He made the effort every day, to visit with her a spell,
To mention how his day had gone, and other things to tell.
It didn't matter how tired he was, or how the weather fared.
Cause whenever he could show up, it showed how much he cared.
Then one day he came in late, bone tired and pert near spent.
His mind was a little confused at first, then his heart became content,
As he sat there and told her, how he missed her so,
And that he wanted to stay right forever, he didn't want to go.
The years were much too lonely now, without her every day.
The tears ran down his weathered face, even more it seemed, today.
He bowed his old gray head, and sought his Master's heart.
"The time has finally come," he said, "from this earth to depart."
And head on home to be with her, the other part of his soul,
Cause when they were together again, they would both be made whole.
And that's just where they found him, lying next to her stone,
For God had joined them once again, now both were finally home.

In Texas, we take our honky tonks serious. Blanco's has been a quite place (only at certain times!) where I have written some of my best stuff, at least in my opinion ! It is a landmark in the Texas Country Music scene and, if you're ever in Houston, you should put it on your "must see" agenda! Howdy, you all !

RIVER OAKS HONKY TONK
(BLANCO'S)

When you hear of honky tonks, ice houses and friendly folks,
The first place you think of, usually ain't River Oaks!

But if you're lookin' to have fun, and hear good music, too.
Listen to this ole cowboy, he'll tell you what to do.

Go on down down to Blanco's, in the heart of Houston town.
And you'll have been to the best honky tonk, for miles and miles around.

It ain't big or fancy, no pretense accepted there.
Just the best live music, good folks and cold, cold beer.

A toss at the antlers, will win you a cheer or two,
And a short bit of fame, for at least a minute or two.

The regulars are from all over, moneyed or poor as dirt.
But most will treat you right, some from their backs, give you their shirt.

You can go in for a hot lunch, the "Special" is always best,
Whether jalapeno sausage, or skillet fried chicken breast.

The girls will make you feel welcome, Karen, Gail and
   Raul, too!
Don't ask about the last one, he doesn't have a clue!

But the place will wrap around you, you'll get to feelin'
   fine.
The name out front is "Blanco's", a rose is on the sign.

So just come on over for a beer, or the music, or to meet
   a friend.
The door is always open, just bring yourself right on in!

You can come in your pickup truck, Mercedes, Ford or
   Lexus,
To the "Honky Tonkin'est Beer Joint, In River Oaks
   Texas!

Sometimes we forget what was done to secure our freedom. My ancestor, David Crockett, still lives because of his contribution to Texas. Thanks, great, great, great granddad.

SACRIFICE

The sounds of the battle were now sounds of pain,
From the wounded and dying, who had so much to gain.

The fate of ole Texas, had hung on the scale.
And the courage of Sam Houston, future legends would tell.

How the Texians had triumphed, at San Jacinto that day.

And avenged the Alamo and Goliad that's what history would say.

Now over many years, we look into the past.
And there remains a question, our heroes would ask.

Have we forgotten, the places and names of those men,
Who gave Texas their all, through the cannons loud din?

Yes, some have forgotten, but many honor them today.
As we stand here together, here is what we must say,

"Ole Texas is still proud, and she still remains free,
And to the Fathers of Texas, we owe it all to thee!

Talk about rememberin'! These are as fresh as when they happened.

THE LONG ROAD HOME

The longest trail often begins, with the cinch brought up tight.
And goes on for days and days, and many lonely nights.

Miles of heat and dust, and cold and wet winter's long.
Your horse becomes your closest friend, the creak of saddle leather, your song.

Those days of mendin' fences, with cuts and calluses hard.
You spent those long days alone, horse and dog became your pards.

Miles spent out lookin' for strays, and bringing them all back in.
The campfires under God's starlit sky, into our memories, seem to blend.

Ole Shorty's snorin' at night, in the bunkhouse on the northern range.
He's seven years gone now, without him sure seems strange.

The kid who broke the horses, a buckaroo, young and strong.
I can't remember his name right now, has it really been that long?

And that line shack on the summer pasture, small but a cowboy's home.
Each day was dawn to sunset, as the wide country we did roam.

And as the years have gone by, our hair turned from brown to grey.
We must be getting' older, what a strange thing for us to say!

For time has crept up on us, as we worked and rode the miles.
We seem to have forgotten the hard times, for now we just have smiles,

That crease our eyes and faces, the wrinkles we've surely earned,
And from life's long textbook, many so hard to learn.

So, it's almost time to unsaddle, and loosen up the cinch,
And take some time to sit down, with our memories, on the bench,

That sits outside our cabin, by the creek from so long ago.
Enjoying the final ride with them, and goin' with the flow!

A word of explanation is in order for most folks so's this story will make sense. Prior to the formation of the American Quarter Horse Association in 1939, the "type" horse that became the Quarter Horse was widely referred to as a "Steel Dust", or "Dust" for short. With that bein' said, the story about a cowboy's luck at playin' poker, will make a whole lot more sense.

THE HAND

He sits and wonders,
'Bout the way things was a goin'.

And comes to the conclusion,
That he shoulda been knowin',

That even with the money left,
In his pockets and his 'roll.
He couldn't get far,
Cause his saddle and horse was sold.

Dog gonedest thing he'd ever seen.
A good hand at stud, a straight.
Been playin' cards for hours long,
Part drunk, was getting' late.

So he took a chance, what the heck.
He was at least even, he thought.
And the way his luck was runnin',
He could take this final pot!

But his cash was shy for the call,
The Steel Dust was all he had.
Could he find a buyer?
Of course, but it was really sad,

That on a simple straight,
This cowboy bet his all.
And came up a little short,
Four aces, the final call.

So he sits and waits and wonders,
About the way things had gone.
And hears that far off coyote,
Who sings that lonely call.

Another day will soon be here.
And he'll find a job, he's hopin',
Stringin' fence and tossin' hay,
Brandin' calves and steers a ropin'

But one thing he's learned for sure,
Is not to drink and play,
At cards for long, or for his 'Dust
A high price he had paid!

Think back. Didn't you know someone like this?

HER SMILE

I seen many a pretty sight, in my years of runnin' round.
But I saw a smile yesterday, that knocked me to the
   ground.

Now, I ain't no innocent, who's never traveled far from
   this place.
But I've never seen a smile so sweet, as on that lovely
   face.

Her hair under a ball cap, a pony tail in back.
The sparkle in her eyes and that smile, Lord please!
   Cut me some slack!

Her laughter like an angels, the notes always so sweet.
It made the perfect package, this ole cowboy'd like to
   keep!

But all that's on the outside, there more kept under
   wraps,
And if you simply listen, her wisdom she will share,
   perhaps.

Now I know you think I'm lyin', stretchin' the truth a
   might.
But I ain't got the words, if I wrote into the night.

So let's just leave it simple, and tell it plain and true.
She makes this cowboy feel four square, a happy
   buckaroo!

JUST CALL ME "W"

Years were spent in getting' ready, for those days that were to come.
He knew that trouble was a comin', and he'd be ready for some.

"They" said he had no "Gravi Tas", little did they know,
He was a man of deep convictions, his character time would show,

That he stood for all Americans, and all that is right and true.
When the time came for action, he'd know just what to do.

Waverin' wasn't his style at all, he always knew where he stood.
Mom and dad had raised him right, he'd turned out pretty good!

Well, we in Texas, knew he was good. We let him run our state.
And when he ran for President, it was really great!

But those knuckle heads in Florida, kept it in the air.
And the victory was slow in comin', hangin' chads we would not share!

"HE WON!" it was shouted, "and so did you and me.
But dark clouds were 'a comin', those clouds from oe'r the sea.

Then came September 11, everything was to change.
Our world was turned upside down, and everything rearranged.

Now was the time to stand tall, and W surely did.
The rats would scurry for their holes, and Osama surely did!

The time for decision was now at hand, what were we to
   do.
Ol W said, "this is war!" "and our forces we will move."

So new names we had to learn right quick, and how to
   say them right,
We saw our soldiers on TV, each and every night.

The war will continue, he said, till terrorism is finally
   defeated.
And our brave soldiers over there, we must sacrifice
   what is needed.

W is showin' us the way, but we must also lead,
And stand our ground together, the warnings we
   must heed.

The price of freedom is vigilance, and the strength to
   defend our own,
Against those who hate us for, the peace that we have
   sown.

W is a man standing, as a representative of our land.
It's a right thing to do, beside him we must stand,

Yet there are those who want to see, W stumble and fail.
But they are only after power, so lies they seem to tell.

W is trying to keep us safe and bring peace back to
   our land.
So, let's remember that old rally cry, "United We Stand"

"Come with me to those thrilling days of yester-year, when ….". Do you remember when you heard that before one of your favorite westerns began? Yes, The Lone Ranger was one of the best and left a lasting memory on many of us as kids. But, then again, so did a lot of cowboys and cowgirls. Roy Rogers and Dale Evans, Hoppalong Cassity, The Cisco Kid and Pancho, The Lone Ranger and Tonto, Sky King and Penny, John Wayne, Jimmie Stewart, Henry Fonda, all made us look forward to Saturday mornings.

At first it was the movie theater down town, the "Silver Screen". Then the "Silver Screen" became that new fangled television. We would sit, in our pajamas, eating cereal, watchin' our heroes fight the bad guys and always win. Kinda left you with a good feelin', didn't it?

But, nothin' could ever compare to the one, true original "Silver Screen", the movie theater!

So, kids, "Come with me to those thrilling days of yester-year "

THE SILVER SCREEN

The names I seem to remember best, from when I was a kid,
Are now the stuff of legends telling, of the daring deeds they did.

T.V. wasn't the way at first, we saw our heroes then.
The Silver Screen on Saturdays, was where it all began.

A nickel or dime was entrance fee, a coke a nickel more.
And our feet would always stick, on that gooey movie floor.

The guys would always laugh and talk, then the lights were turned down low.
To signal all was to begin soon, the start of our favorite shows.

The serial was continued from last week. Could the hero
   come back again?
And if he was dumb enough to kiss the girl, all of us
   would grin.

Now was time for the western to start, we all could
   hardly wait.
Then Dale and Roy and Trigger were there, ridin'
   through the gate.

And Roy was oh so smooth, as he sang a cowboy song.
We kids knew every single word, so we would sing
   along.

Next week it might be Hoppalong, or the Cisco Kid.
Everyone really loved those guys, and the daring deeds
   they did.

Gene Autry was a favorite, and Champion his trusty
   steed.
When he told us to follow "The Cowboy Code", we
   were quick to heed.

The Lone Ranger with Tonto his trusted friend, kept us
   glued there in our seats.
They may have been my favorites, I dreamed someday
   we'd meet!

His silver bullets never failed, to find the bad guys
   hearts.
Many ran when they heard his name, headin' for other
   parts.

John Wayne, The Duke some called him, fought for
   right in every show.
Another of our cowboy heroes, pointing the way to go.

Now there's a Silver Screen's in every home, both here
   and in far off lands.
But some have never seen those guys, ridin' 'cross the
   sands.

I think it's time we brought them back, those heroes
   from long ago,
And they would straighten out the world, the right way
   they would show.

And we could all be kids again, knowing who was really
   bad and mean,
The world would be a better place again, if we had that
   "Silver Screen"!

After many a mistake in the field of marryin', this ol cowboy had pert near given up. However, if anyone doubts that we have a God of miracles, my meetin' "Miss Judy", a school marm, proves that He still does BIG ones, even in this modern world. Personally, I thought those miracles were for everybody else. But He musta wanted to show everyone that He even does 'em for "good ol boys", too! I wrote this for my bride on our weddin' day and stumbled through it with a big ol lump in my throat. I reckon if it don't do something to you, too, you must be dead. I share this with you, because it may give you hope, too!

A WEDDING PROMISE

I've traveled down the long road called life,
Stumblin', trippin' and slidin' most of the way.
And I'd just about given up hope of findin' someone.
I thought I was at the end of my day.

Then God smiled on His buckaroo son,
Down in Texas, His heaven on earth.
And gave me a love I can hardly believe.
No money can measure her worth.

Her smile is like the sun on a stream,
On a sparkling, clear summer day.
And her eyes really twinkle when she looks at me,
With my mind she like to play.

I've done nothin' to deserve the love she gives,
  I tell her most every day.
She replies I do more than she can ever explain,
  Then smiles and that's all she will say.

So, today I freely give her my ol heart,
  The only one she seems to need.
And carry her into the rest of our lives,
  Her wisdom I will carefully heed.

Thank you, my love, for taking me,
To the place I've always wanted to be.
With my one true love here beside me,
  Our future is bright, wait and see!

Lloyd "RAINMAN" Shelby
CowBiography

"This cowboy doesn't know of another poet or picker working harder, or more devoted to bringing what cowboy was, and is, to the American people. Lloyd embodies the western genre as it embodies him." Curly Musgrave, WMA Male Performer of the Year and Songwriter of the Year 2002.

"Do you hear the distant rumbling of the thunder? You can if you listen to the Rainman. Drawing the listener into his world, Lloyd Shelby breathes life into the characters of this magnificent album of Western poetry. It serves as a classic example of the genre and will stand for generations. Come to where the visions of the past are as real as you and I. Listen...hear the thunder...smell the rain." Debra Coppinger Hill – Host and Executive Producer of "Love of The West", Academy of Western Artist Cowgirl Poet of the Year 2002.

Lloyd Shelby is a Texan, first, last and always. He was raised in Texas and Oklahoma during the last century with Roy and Dale, Gene Autry, Hoppy, The Duke, Dale Robertson, and all the rest of the silver screen cowboys. However, **Lloyd** lived the cowboy life by training horses, being a farrier (ask, if you don't know what that is!), and attending Agricultural school at Oklahoma State.

He began writing early in his life and never stopped. A brief time spent on the East coast broke him of leaving Texas for too long and he now lives in Crosby, Texas on the well know "R Bar P Ranch", known by locals as the Rancho Pequito, where he still raises and trains horses and a small herd of mosquitoes.

Lloyd has performed at all places great and small, from groups around an evening campfire to The National Cowboy Hall of Fame and The Bob Bullock Texas State History Museum in Austin. His syndicated weekly column "Horsefeathers" has a large following as he expounds on subjects from Iraq ("if Iraq, you break") to local heroes and poetry, all from the wizened perspective of a cowboy. He started acting when he was small and has performed at the Houston Music Theater and numerous other small theaters in Texas.

Recently, **Lloyd** produced and co-starred in a stage show with his friends, Jim "Curly" Musgrave and the renowned Linda Kirkpatrick, appropriately titled, "A Cowboy True". The reception for this first of its kind production was overwhelming and the show is scheduled to be presented at several venues around Texas.

The Academy of Western Artists awarded "*Rainman*", **Lloyd**'s second book, its first ever Will Rogers Medallion Award in 2002. The CD of the same name has received critical acclaim and was nominated for Poetry CD of the Year by the AWA for 2003. For 2003, he was also been nominated for Rising Star, Storyteller/Humor and Male Poet of The Year. **Lloyd** is the Official Cowboy Poet for the world famous George Ranch in Richmond, Texas

Lloyd writes about the personal parts of a cowboy's life and loves and he enjoys touching the soft spot in all of us. "Our job as poets and performers is to evoke feelings, real emotions, from our audiences and readers. If we put our own passion into our work, others should be able to feel it as we do."

"Cowboy Kids" is a program **Lloyd** has started in Texas to work with fourth through seventh graders. Cowboy Kids works through the local school districts to promote our Texas and cowboy heritage and to encourage the students in their writing skills, specifically poetry of the cowboy genre. A website is being developed as a database and showcase of students poetry to be used by schools throughout the state.

Lloyd is known for his dramatic, epic stories about early Texas and the famed Texas Rangers, as well as his heart warming poems of his animals and loves. Young and old alike enjoy this "descendent of Davy Crockett" and his warm style.

You'll enjoy **Lloyd** at your next shindig, large or small! For information about availability and bookings, or to purchase Lloyd's books and CD's, contact:

Lloyd Shelby
Painted Word Studios
P.O. Box 1606
Crosby, Texas 77532

Phone: 1 866 241-7510

E-Mail: lloydshelby@ev1.net   www.paintedwordstudios.com

Harris County Public Library
Houston, Texas